FOOTBALL'S GREATEST STARS

Michael Hurley

www.heinemannlibrary.co.uk
Visit our website to find out more information about Heinemann Library books.

To order:
☎ Phone +44 (0) 1865 888066
▤ Fax +44 (0) 1865 314091
⌨ Visit www.heinemannlibrary.co.uk

Heinemann Library is an imprint of Capstone Global Library Limited, a company incorporated in England and Wales having its registered office at 7 Pilgrim Street, London, EC4V 6LB - Registered company number: 6695582

"Heinemann" is a registered trademark of Pearson Education Limited, under licence to Capstone Global Library Limited

Edited by Kate de Villiers, Catherine Clarke, and Vaarunika Dharmapala
Designed by Steve Mead and Debbie Oatley
Picture research by Hannah Taylor
Originated by Dot Gradations Ltd
Printed and bound in China by CTPS

ISBN 978 0 431044 37 8 (hardback)
14 13 12 11 10
10 9 8 7 6 5 4 3 2 1

British Library Cataloguing in Publication Data
Hurley, Michael
Football's greatest stars. -- (The World Cup)
796.3'34668-dc22
A full catalogue record for this book is available from the British Library.

Acknowledgements
We would like to thank the following for permission to reproduce photographs: © KPT Power Photos **background image**; Action Images pp. 10 (Richard Heathcote Livepic), 13, 14 (MSI), 15, 18 (Sporting Pictures/Tony Marshall), 27 (Tony O'Brien); Corbis pp. 22 & 23 (TempSport/© Christian Liewig); Getty Images pp. 4 & 5 (Popperfoto), 7 (Popperfoto/Rolls Press), 9 & 21 (AFP), 16 (Hulton Archive), 19 (AFP/Damien Meyer), 20 & 24 (Bob Thomas); PA Photos pp. 11 (S&G and Barratts), 17 & 26 (© Empics/Peter Robinson); Reuters pp. 6 (Roberto Jayme), 12 (Chor Sokunthea), 25 (Action Images/Jordan Murph); Shutterstock pp. 28 & 29 (© Gordan), **background image** (© Nikola I).

Cover photograph of England vs Japan, International Football friendly match, City of Manchester Stadium, 1st June 2004 reproduced with permission of Rex Features/Jed Leicester.

Every effort has been made to contact copyright holders of material reproduced in this book. Any omissions will be rectified in subsequent printings if notice is given to the publisher.

CONTENTS

Some words are shown in the text in bold, **like this**.
You can find out what they mean by looking in the
glossary on page 31.

THE WORLD CUP

The first ever **FIFA** World Cup was held in 1930. There have been 18 World Cup **tournaments**. The first World Cup was held in Uruguay, in South America. Uruguay hosted the tournament because they were the current Olympic football champions. National teams from around the world were invited to take part. Only 13 teams played in the 1930 World Cup. These teams included France, Brazil, Argentina, and the United States. Uruguay beat Argentina in the final.

The 2010 World Cup will be held in South Africa and will feature 32 teams. It is the first time that the competition has been held in Africa.

Football's greatest stars

The 1958 World Cup was the sixth World Cup tournament. It was held in Sweden, in Europe. A brilliant Brazil team won this tournament. Brazil had a 17-year-old **forward** called Pelé. Pelé had a fantastic tournament. He scored six goals: two of them in the final. Pelé went on to play for Brazil at three more World Cups. He was probably the first real football star. He was famous throughout the world… and still is!

France's Just Fontaine also had a very successful tournament in 1958. He finished as top goal scorer with 13 goals. His record for goals scored in a World Cup still stands today. The World Cup has seen many great players since that 1958 tournament.

A crowd of 80,000 at the Montevideo Estadio Centenario watched the first ever World Cup final in 1930.

PELÉ
(BRAZIL)

STATS

DATE OF BIRTH: 23/10/1940

POSITION: FORWARD

WORLD CUP APPEARANCES: 14

WORLD CUP GOALS: 12

Edson Arantes do Nascimento is better known to football fans around the world as Pelé. Pelé played in four **FIFA** World Cups and was part of a World Cup winning Brazil team three times. Pelé had amazing football skills. He was quick and strong and had a very powerful **shot**. Pelé was a complete player. This means that he could run, shoot, pass, tackle, and head the ball very well. He could do things with a football that other players could only dream of.

Although Pelé retired from football in 1977, he is still one of the most famous footballers in the world. This photograph was taken in 2008, at the opening of an exhibition about his life.

Pelé was only 17 years old when he played in his first World Cup in 1958. Even then, he was Brazil's star player. Pelé's goals helped Brazil win their first World Cup. The World Cup in 1966, however, was not very successful for Brazil and Pelé. Brazil went out of the **tournament** at the first stage, after Pelé was injured.

World Cup 1970

After disappointment in 1966, Brazil were determined to regain the title of world champions. Pelé was in his late twenties. He had matured into a truly great footballer. He was captain of his country and their most important player.

The Brazil team at the 1970 World Cup has been described by football fans as the greatest football team ever, and Pelé as the greatest player ever. Pelé played in every Brazil match at the 1970 World Cup. He scored four goals. One of these goals was in the final **versus** Italy. Brazil won the match 4–1 to become world champions again.

The 1970 World Cup was a success for Brazil and Pelé.

GARRINCHA
(BRAZIL)

Garrincha played for Brazil at three **FIFA** World Cups. He was part of the Brazil team that won the trophy in both 1958 and 1962. Although Garrincha was part of the 1958 Brazil World Cup squad, he did not play in their first two matches. He was brought into the Brazil team for their last group match and played well enough to stay in the team for the rest of the **tournament**. He went on to play in three more matches, including the final.

STATS

DATE OF BIRTH: 28/10/1933

POSITION: WINGER

WORLD CUP APPEARANCES: 11

WORLD CUP GOALS: 5

Garrincha helped Brazil win their first World Cup. Brazil had the two greatest players of the time: Garrincha and Pelé. Garrincha was a different type of player from Pelé: he was a **winger**. He had amazing **dribbling** skills. He was quick and could run past **defenders** with the ball at his feet. It often looked as though the ball was glued to his boots. His dribbling ability was possibly the best ever.

Goals galore

In the 1962 World Cup Garrincha was Brazil's best player. When Pelé was injured in Brazil's first match, many supporters thought that Brazil could not win the tournament. Garrincha had other ideas. He was amazing, scoring goals and creating goals for other players. At the 1962 World Cup he scored four goals in six matches, and was officially named as the best player of the tournament. He was also the joint top goal scorer. He had proved that Brazil could win without Pelé.

Garrincha (left) dribbles the ball easily past a Welsh defender in the 1958 World Cup quarter-final.

Little Bird

Garrincha's real name was Manoel Francisco dos Santos. Because he was small his sister gave him the nickname Garrincha, which means "Little Bird". As well as being small, Garrincha was also unusual because his legs were different lengths. When he was a teenager many experts thought he would never be able to play professional football. This didn't stop Little Bird!

EUSEBIO
(PORTUGAL)

Eusebio is the greatest player in the history of Portuguese football. Born in Mozambique, Africa, Eusebio moved to Portugal when he was 18 years old. He made his **debut** for Portugal a year later and went on to play for them 64 times. Eusebio only played in one **FIFA** World Cup, in England in 1966. Eusebio was one of the stars of the **tournament**, and was the top goal scorer with nine goals.

STATS

DATE OF BIRTH: 25/01/1942

POSITION: FORWARD

WORLD CUP APPEARANCES: 6

WORLD CUP GOALS: 9

Eusebio's club team was Benfica. This statue of him stands outside Benfica's stadium in Lisbon, Portugal, as a reminder of their greatest ever player.

Golden Player

The Portuguese Football Federation named Eusebio their "Golden Player" in 2004 to celebrate 50 years of **UEFA**.

Important goals

Eusebio was a **forward** with lots of **pace** and strength. He also had a very powerful **shot**. His performances in the 1966 World Cup were very good. He helped his team by scoring some vital goals. Portugal won their first match 3–1 and then in the second match Eusebio scored one of the goals as they beat Bulgaria 3–0. Eusebio's goal-scoring form carried into the final group match **versus** Brazil. He scored twice as Portugal knocked the World Cup holders out of the tournament.

Portugal's quarter-final match was against North Korea. Portugal were expected to beat the Koreans. After 25 minutes Eusebio and his teammates found themselves 3–0 down. Eusebio then scored four goals to help his team win the match 5–3. It was an incredible individual performance by the young forward.

This was just one of the goals that Eusebio scored against North Korea to **inspire** his team to come back and win the match.

In the semi-final against England, Portugal lost 2–1. Eusebio played well and scored a **penalty** in the last 10 minutes, but it wasn't enough to see his team through to the final. He also scored in the playoff match against the Soviet Union – the other losing semi-finalists. Portugal clinched third place in the World Cup with a 2–1 victory. Eusebio had scored nine goals in six matches. He had also captured the imagination of football fans around the world.

BOBBY CHARLTON [ENGLAND]

England's Bobby Charlton was an outstanding midfielder, and he had a very successful football career. He played more than 100 times for his country and was part of the England team that won the **FIFA** World Cup in 1966. He is also England's all-time top goal scorer with 49 goals. Charlton played for England in three World Cups and scored four goals. His performances in 1966 were crucial to England's success.

Sir Bobby Charlton is involved in charity work, such as raising awareness for a landmine charity here in Cambodia.

STATS

DATE OF BIRTH: 11/10/1937

POSITION: MIDFIELDER

WORLD CUP APPEARANCES: 12

WORLD CUP GOALS: 4

Sir Bobby

As well as being a great player for England, Bobby Charlton was also a great club player. He played for Manchester United for 17 years. He won the **UEFA** European Cup and the English league championship three times. In 1994, Charlton was given a **knighthood** by the Queen for his services to football and charity. His official title is Sir Bobby Charlton.

Along with his 1966 teammates, Bobby Charlton (top right) will always be remembered for England's World Cup victory.

England's greatest moment

Bobby Charlton was a very **consistent** player for club and country. He was always willing to attack the **opposition** and shoot from a distance. Charlton's powerful **shots** were very popular with fans. He scored twice against Portugal in the World Cup semi-final in 1966, and England won that match 2–1. He then helped England to beat West Germany in the final. He didn't score, but he worked very hard for his team, trying to stop the German attacks. His reward was a World Cup winners medal and he will always be associated with the greatest result in the history of English football.

After finishing his playing career Bobby Charlton has continued to be involved in football. He created football schools to help children improve their skills and he has worked as an **ambassador** for English football. Like Pelé, he is recognized throughout the world by football fans.

FRANZ BECKENBAUER
(WEST GERMANY)

Franz Beckenbauer made his **debut** for West Germany in 1965 when he was only 20 years old. He went on to win more than 100 **caps** for his country. Beckenbauer played in three **FIFA** World Cups for West Germany, in 1966, 1970, and 1974, and made 18 appearances. He was a strong, powerful **defender** with good ball control and passing ability.

STATS

DATE OF BIRTH: 11/09/1945

POSITION: DEFENDER

WORLD CUP APPEARANCES: 18

WORLD CUP GOALS: 5

Franz Beckenbauer (in white) challenges for the ball against Holland at the 1974 World Cup.

Beckenbauer's first World Cup appearance was against Switzerland in 1966. He scored two goals in a convincing 5–0 win. As a defender Beckenbauer was not expected to score as many goals as he did. He had a good **tournament** in 1966, where he scored goals in the quarter-final and semi-final before West Germany were beaten by England in the final.

At the 1970 World Cup, Beckenbauer and West Germany made it to the semi-finals, but were beaten by Italy. In 1974 the World Cup was held in West Germany and Beckenbauer's team were one of the favourites. West Germany were the **hosts**, and there was a lot of pressure on Beckenbauer and his teammates. The German fans expected them to win the tournament. With Beckenbauer controlling the play, West Germany coped very well with this added pressure. They made it to the final where they beat Holland 2–1 in a close match.

Player and manager

Franz Beckenbauer is one of only two men to have won the World Cup as a player and also as a manager. He was captain of the West Germany team that won the tournament in 1974 on home soil. He was the manager of West Germany in 1990 when they beat Argentina in the final.

Beckenbauer (second from top-left) poses with his team as it celebrates winning the World Cup in 1990.

Der Kaiser

Franz Beckenbauer was given the nickname "Der Kaiser" in the late 1960s. It is German for "The Emperor". This name was meant to describe his **influence** and control on the football pitch.

JOHAN CRUYFF
(HOLLAND)

Johan Cruyff is Holland's most famous, skilful, and **influential** player ever. He had wonderful balance and great ball control. He was able to pass precisely, shoot accurately, and **dribble** the ball confidently. Cruyff made his club **debut** for Ajax, in Holland, when he was only 17 years old and made his debut for his national team soon after.

STATS

DATE OF BIRTH: 25/04/1947

POSITION: FORWARD

WORLD CUP APPEARANCES: 7

WORLD CUP GOALS: 3

Holland's star player

Cruyff's greatest moment as a player was during the 1974 World Cup in West Germany. Although Holland ended the **tournament** as runners-up, the team played brilliant football that was popular with fans. In a team full of technically good players, Cruyff was the star. He roamed around the pitch causing trouble for the **opposition**, switching positions with his teammates to make the most of his attacking talents.

Even as a very young player, Johan Cruyff (far right) was a star for his club, Ajax.

Cruyff scored some memorable goals during the tournament. He scored two of his team's four goals against Argentina in a 4–0 win. He then scored the second goal of the match when Holland beat Brazil 2–0, hitting a stunning **volley** into the net. After the win against Brazil, Holland were in the World Cup final, where they met the **hosts** West Germany. Cruyff earned his team a **penalty** in the first few minutes of the final. He was fouled as he dribbled the ball into the penalty area, and Holland took a 1–0 lead from the penalty spot. West Germany scored two goals to take the lead. Although Holland, with Cruyff trying his hardest, continued to play skilful, attacking football they could not get back into the match. Holland were beaten 2–1.

Holland and Ajax's greatest ever player

Johan Cruyff was Holland's most important player during the 1970s. He was also the most important player for his club, Ajax. Ajax won the **UEFA** European Cup three times in a row, in 1971, 1972, and 1973.

MICHEL PLATINI
(FRANCE)

Michel Platini was one the greatest footballers ever. He played exceptional football to help his team France to the **FIFA** World Cup semi-finals twice: in 1982 and 1986. Platini was a very skilful midfielder. His passing ability was outstanding and he scored some fantastic goals from **free kicks**.

STATS

DATE OF BIRTH: 21/06/1955
POSITION: MIDFIELDER
WORLD CUP APPEARANCES: 14
WORLD CUP GOALS: 5

Michel Platini made his World Cup **debut** in 1978, but France could not advance past the group stage. Platini and France had a more successful World Cup in 1982. They were unlucky to lose on **penalties** against West Germany in the semi-final. Platini was one of the best players at the **tournament**. He used his skills and intelligence on the pitch to create opportunities for his teammates.

Platini plays for his country at the 1986 World Cup.

France's most important player

In 1986, in Mexico, France were one of the favourites for the World Cup. Platini had matured into a world-class midfielder and wanted to help his team win the trophy for the first time. France performed brilliantly during the tournament. Platini was the most important player in a very **creative** French midfield. He scored goals in wins against Italy and Brazil, two of the other tournament favourites. France met West Germany again in the semi-final. France lost 2–0 and they were out of the World Cup. When Platini retired from playing football, at 32 years of age, he had won every trophy available in his career except the World Cup.

Staying in football

After his career as a player finished, Michel Platini was the manager of France between 1988 and 1992. He worked on the organizing committee of the 1998 World Cup in France. He has also worked as an advisor to Sepp Blatter, the president of FIFA. Platini is now the president of **UEFA**, the Union of European Football Associations.

As UEFA president, Platini presented the Spain team with their medals after they won the Euro 2008 championship.

DIEGO MARADONA
[ARGENTINA]

Diego Maradona's football career was full of amazing moments and **controversy**. Maradona played for Argentina at four **FIFA** World Cups, playing in 21 matches. He was part of the Argentina team that won the World Cup in Mexico in 1986, and was a losing finalist four years later in Italy.

STATS

DATE OF BIRTH: 30/10/1960

POSITION: MIDFIELDER

WORLD CUP APPEARANCES: 21

WORLD CUP GOALS: 8

Maradona made his first appearance at a World Cup in 1982, in Spain. He scored his first World Cup goal in a group match, **versus** Hungary. Argentina failed to get beyond the second round and Maradona was sent off in their match against Brazil.

Winning the World Cup

The World Cup in 1986 was much more successful for Argentina and Maradona in particular. Fans watched as the stocky little midfielder used his incredible **dribbling** skills and wonderful balance to defeat the **opposition**.

Maradona and his team celebrate winning the World Cup in 1986. ➜

In the quarter-final against England, Maradona scored both of his team's goals in a 2–1 win. The first was very controversial because he used his hand to score. The goal should have been disallowed. The second goal was one of the greatest ever scored in a World Cup match. Maradona ran half the length of the pitch and dribbled the ball past six England players before slotting the ball into the goal to score. He had another excellent match against Belgium in the semi-final, scoring twice to take his team into the final.

Argentina beat West Germany 3–2 in the final to win the World Cup. Diego Maradona was named the player of the **tournament** for his amazing performances.

After some thrilling performances in the World Cup in 1986 and 1990 Diego Maradona was sent home in disgrace from the 1994 World Cup in the United States. He was banned from playing football because he failed a drugs test. Maradona has always been a controversial figure, but his brilliant ability as a footballer has never been in doubt.

"Goal of the Century"

In a poll on FIFA's website Diego Maradona's second goal against England in the 1986 World Cup was voted by fans as the "Goal of the Century".

ZINEDINE ZIDANE
(FRANCE)

Zinedine Zidane is one of the greatest footballers of recent times. He played for France at three **FIFA** World Cups. He was the most important and **influential** player for France when they won the World Cup at home in 1998. He was also part of the France team that lost in the final to Italy in 2006.

Fans around the world think of Zidane as one of the most skilful players to have ever played football. He had great balance, **vision**, and passing ability. His performances for France in 1998 were very important to the team's success. France made it through to the semi-finals after beating Italy on **penalties**. Because France were playing at home, there was a lot of pressure on the players to succeed.

France made it to the final after a close semi-final match with Croatia that they won 2–1. Zidane did not score but his calm, confident performance helped his teammates to do well. In the final against Brazil, Zidane was again the most important player for France. He scored two goals in a convincing 3–0 win and he was named as the **man of the match** in the World Cup final. The French fans celebrated their team's first ever World Cup win.

STATS

DATE OF BIRTH: 23/06/1972

POSITION: MIDFIELDER

WORLD CUP APPEARANCES: 12

WORLD CUP GOALS: 5

Sent off in disgrace

The 2006 final was Zidane's last appearance for France and the midfielder's brilliant career ended in **controversy** when he was sent off. He made headlines around the world for all of the wrong reasons when he head-butted an **opponent** in the chest and was given a **red card**. Despite being sent off in the final, Zidane's fantastic performances meant that he was named player of the **tournament**.

Zidane celebrates after scoring the second goal of the 1998 World Cup final against Brazil.

World Player of the Year

Zinedine Zidane was named the FIFA World Player of the Year three times in his career. The only other player to have achieved this is Brazil's Ronaldo.

DAVID BECKHAM
[ENGLAND]

David Beckham is probably the most famous and popular footballer in the world. He has played more than 100 times for England and has played in three **FIFA** World Cups. Beckham is famous for his ability to cross and shoot the ball accurately. He is also famous for his lifestyle away from football.

David Beckham made his first World Cup appearance in France in 1998. He announced his football ability to fans around the world by scoring a fantastic goal from a **free kick** against Colombia in England's final group match. In the next match, against Argentina, he helped to set up an England goal with a precise pass. The score was 2–2 at half-time. Very early in the second half David Beckham was fouled and he reacted badly. He was sent off for kicking an **opponent**. England failed to beat Argentina with only 10 players on the pitch. They lost on **penalties** and Beckham was devastated.

Beckham helped England get past the group stage at the 1998 World Cup by scoring this free kick against Colombia. It was his first goal for England.

World Cup revenge

David Beckham was blamed for England's failure to beat Argentina. His response was to prove that he was a great player and important for England. His performances improved and he became a vital player for England for the next 10 years. He was made the England captain in 2001.

Beckham was England captain during the 2002 and 2006 World Cup **tournaments**. He scored an important penalty against Argentina at the group stage in 2002, and England won the match 1–0. He was able to get some revenge after his error in 1998. Unfortunately for Beckham he never had the chance to lift the World Cup trophy as England captain. England failed to get past the quarter-finals in 2002 and 2006.

Beckham's football schools

David Beckham has set up two football schools: one in London, England, and another in Los Angeles, USA. These schools aim to develop the skills of young players – the football stars of the future!

As well as his football schools, Beckham takes part in charity and community events, such as this one in Hawaii, to encourage youth football.

OTHER GREAT PLAYERS

Many great footballers have played at the **FIFA** World Cup. Unfortunately, some other great players haven't had the chance to shine at the World Cup. Here are just three of them:

George Best (Northern Ireland)

George Best played football between 1963 and 1984 and was one of the greatest players in the world. He had amazing **dribbling** skills and could score fantastic goals. He could score with either foot, or with his head. Northern Ireland did not qualify for the World Cup when he was an international player. It is a shame that more fans did not get to see this skilful player in action at a World Cup.

Despite being one of the most talented footballers ever, George Best was never able to shine with his Northern Ireland team at a World Cup.

Eric Cantona [France]

Eric Cantona was a skilful, powerful, and confident **forward**. He scored many great goals in his football career. He played for France between 1987 and 1994. Cantona did not have the chance to play in a World Cup because France did not qualify for the **tournament** in 1990 and 1994.

Ryan Giggs [Wales]

Ryan Giggs is the most successful footballer to play in the English Premier League. He has won the league title with his team, Manchester United, 11 times. He has also won the European Cup twice. He has been an important player for his club and his country for a long time. Giggs tried to help Wales qualify for the World Cup many times, but even with his skills and experience they did not succeed.

Ryan Giggs and Eric Cantona enjoyed a lot of success with their club Manchester United.

Common ground

As well as not having the chance to appear at the World Cup, George Best, Eric Cantona, and Ryan Giggs have something else in common. They have all played for Manchester United. Manchester United is one of the most famous and successful football clubs in the world.

There are too many players who have been outstanding performers at the World Cup to mention all of them in this book. Each country that has been represented at the World Cup has had great players showing their abilities to fans all around the world. This is an example of a possible World Cup **All-Star 11**. See page 30 for ways to find out more about these amazing players.

1 Dino Zoff
(Italy)
Date of birth: 28/02/1942
Position: Goalkeeper
World Cup appearances: 17
World Cup goals: 0

2 Bobby Moore
(England)
Date of birth: 12/04/1941
Position: **Defender**
World Cup appearances: 12
World Cup Goals: 0

3 Franz Beckenbauer
(West Germany)
Date of birth: 11/09/1945
Position: Defender
World Cup appearances: 18
World Cup goals: 5

4 Franco Baresi
(Italy)
Date of birth: 08/05/1960
Position: Defender
World Cup appearances: 10
World Cup goals: 0

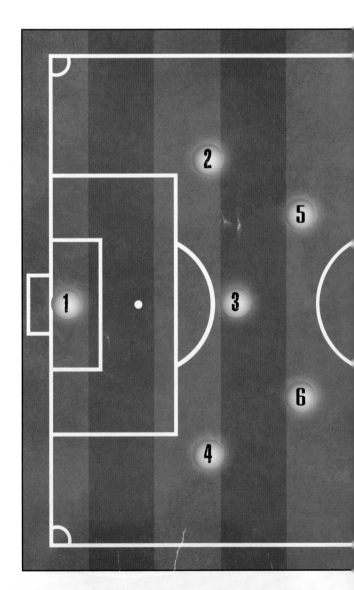

5　Zinedine Zidane
(France)

Date of birth: 23/06/1972
Position: Midfielder
World Cup appearances: 13
World Cup goals: 3

6　Bobby Charlton
(England)

Date of birth: 11/10/1937
Position: Midfielder
World Cup appearances: 12
World Cup goals: 4

7　Johan Cruyff
(Holland)

Date of birth: 25/04/1947
Position: **Forward**
World Cup appearances: 7
World Cup goals: 3

8　Diego Maradona
(Argentina)

Date of birth: 30/10/1960
Position: Midfielder
World Cup appearances: 21
World Cup goals: 8

9　Ronaldo
(Brazil)

Date of birth: 22/09/1976
Position: Forward
World Cup appearances: 19
World Cup goals: 15

10　Pelé
(Brazil)

Date of birth: 23/10/1940
Position: Forward
World Cup appearances: 13
World Cup goals: 12

11　Gerd Muller
(West Germany)

Date of birth: 03/11/1945
Position: Forward
World Cup appearances: 13
World Cup goals: 14

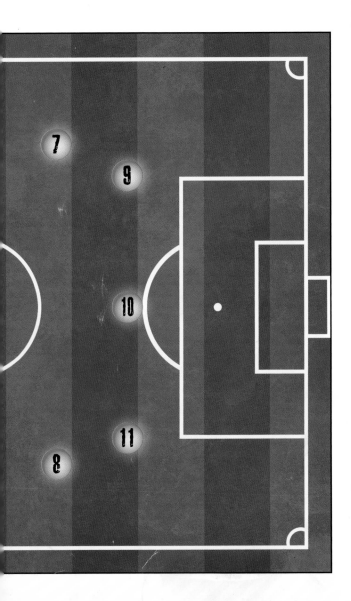

FIND OUT MORE

Books to read

David Beckham: My Side, David Beckham (HarperCollinsWillow, 2004)

*Essential Sports: Football, (*2nd Edition), Andy Smith (Heinemann Library, 2008)

Football: The Ultimate Guide (Dorling Kindersley Publishers Ltd, 2008)

Sport Files: Wayne Rooney, John Townsend (Raintree, 2008)

The Usborne Little Book of Soccer Skills (Usborne Publishing Ltd, 2005)

World Football Stars (Top Trumps), Nick Judd and Tim Dykes (JH Haynes & Co Ltd, 2007)

Websites

www.fifa.com
This website has all of the information about the FIFA World Cup. It is great for finding out about your favourite players and teams.

http://news.bbc.co.uk/sport1/football
You can keep up to date with all the latest football news and match results at the BBC Sports news pages.

GLOSSARY

all-star 11 team containing some of the greatest players ever. An all-star team can include players from different countries who would not normally play on the same side.

ambassador person who represents or raises awareness of an activity. Sports and charities have ambassadors.

cap award given to footballers after playing in each international match

consistent always the same

controversy disagreement. If people disagree with something the referee decides in a football match, it is called a "controversial decision".

creative something new and different

debut first appearance. A footballer's first match is their debut.

defender position of a footballer on the pitch. Defenders try to stop the opposition from scoring.

dribble running with the ball

FIFA (*Fédération Internationale de Football Association*) the international organization responsible for football around the world

forward position of a footballer on the pitch. Forwards try to score goals.

free kick kick of the ball awarded by the referee after a foul. The free kick is given to the team that the foul was committed against.

host in a World Cup tournament, the host is the country where the tournament is being played

influence setting a good example that others want to follow

inspire make people feel that they can do something

knighthood award given out by the Queen of England

man of the match award given after a match to the best player

opposition team that you are playing against

pace speed. A player who has lots of pace can move around the pitch very quickly.

penalty the referee gives a penalty if a foul happens in the 18-yard box. The ball is placed on a spot 12 yards from the goal and only the goalkeeper is allowed to stop the shot.

red card shown by the referee to a player, usually for a dangerous foul. The player has to leave the pitch and their team has to continue with just 10 players.

shot kick of the ball towards the goal

tournament organized number of matches that lead to a final. The winner of the final game wins the tournament.

UEFA (Union of European Football Associations) organization responsible for European football

versus against

vision ability to think about and picture something before it happens

volley kick of the football before it touches the ground

winger position of a player on the pitch. Wingers play wide on the pitch and usually try to create chances for their team to score.

INDEX